Forex: The Simple Strategy on Trading Currency Successfully

Step by Step Guide on Building Wealth Trading on the Foreign Exchange Market

Table of Contents

Introduction

I want to thank you and congratulate you for downloading this book, *"Forex: The Simple Strategy on Trading Currency Successfully"*.

This book contains proven steps and strategies on how to better understand forex trading as an excellent investment alternative. Over the past decade, foreign exchange trading has gained increasing popularity in the investment world all over the globe. Through this book, I hope you will be familiar with the technicalities and effective strategies in forex trading that can let you earn a profit of up to $200 per day.

I encourage you to share this book with your friends and family, and please take the time to write a short review on Amazon to share your thoughts.

Chapter 1: What is Foreign Exchange Trading?

The foreign exchange (forex) market is a global market where one can buy and sell any of the currencies of all countries in the world. The forex market was opened during the 70s with the establishment of free exchange rates. Since that time, the people and businesses who have participated in the forex market have always determined what price one currency will have counter to another currency based on the law of supply and demand. The forex market has always been considered a free trade because it is exempt from any outside control. All those who want to participate in forex trading are free to compete with one another, and they can always choose to enter into a transaction or not.

The huge quantity of forex trading transaction carried out every day in a nonstop movement make the forex market one of the most liquid monetary markets in the world. Based on several research studies, the volume of money traded in the forex market amounts to almost five trillion US dollars per day – not millions, not billions, but *trillions* of dollars. The highest recorded volume of transactions amounts to almost six trillion US dollars in just one day, and the average daily amount of total transactions is around three trillion US dollars. The precise amount cannot really be ascertained because all forex transactions are not completed in one central forex exchange.

You can conduct forex trading from anywhere in the world through both telecommunication networks and the Internet. Unlike the stock market that only operates during the traditional business hours, the forex exchange operates 24 hours a day, five days each week. Forex trading starts at 00:00 GMT on Mondays and ends at 22:00 GMT on Fridays. Wherever you may be, you can always find a dealer who can give you currency quotes in all time zones. The major forex exchanges are located in the following principal markets: Frankfurt and London in Europe, New York in North America, Tokyo and Hong Kong in Asia, and Australia and New Zealand in the Pacific.

The foreign exchange market is capable of maintaining its neutrality and avoiding being controlled by just a few huge participants because of the sheer volume of transactions. Even if there are huge participants who want to control the market by willingly altering the prices, they will be required to invest several billions of US dollars. Unlike the stock market, which can easily crash because of a major economic event, the forex market can easily bounce back after a catastrophic event because of the high volume of money flowing in and out of it every day.

To better understand how forex transactions are quoted, you just need to remember that a base currency is always quoted as a unit equivalent to the exchange rate of the quote currency. For instance, if you see the quote EUR/USD = 1.2762, it means that the base currency is the EUR, and one unit of EUR is equal to 1.2762 USD (which is the quote currency).

Each forex trading transaction is completed through separate contracts, which are also referred to as "lots." The typical size of one contract or lot is 100,000 units. This signifies that if you acquire one typical sized contract, you will be able to control a base currency with a total quantity of 100,000 units. Each contract is then subdivided into "pips," which pertains to the minimum price increment. Standard lots or contracts normally have a pip value of $10, but if you are just starting with forex trading, you can try the mini-accounts that some forex companies offer, wherein the lot size can be as low as 10,000 units with pips amounting to just $1 or even less.

Compared to the stock market, the forex trading market requires quite a lower margin, especially when you know how to take advantage of leverage. In forex trading, you are not obligated to actually purchase a currency, so you are able to trade it a later time. You can technically open a forex position to buy or sell a currency even if you do not own any of that currency. You can open a normal forex account through an Internet broker by setting up a minimum deposit of $2,000. With the minimum deposit, you can start trading in the forex market with a 1:100 leverage. That means that you can open a position amounting to $200,000, but with an investment of only $2,000 and the remaining $298,000 as a credit.

If you do not wish to invest a big amount right away, there are several forex brokers who offer a "mini-account" for a smaller investment amounting to $250. A mini-account can allow you to control up a lot of up to $10,000 units of base currency with a margin deposit of $50 only. This means that you can work with a leverage of 200:1 computed as $10,000 divided by $50. Your $250 minimum investment can then allow you to trade up to five mini-lots. In other instances, the leverage can go as high as 400:1 or even 500:1, which means that you will be required to use a margin deposit lesser than $50.

The leverage you can enjoy in forex trading is around fifty times higher than what stock trading can offer. As mandated by United States laws, you can have an intraday leverage of 4:1 in stock trading if you own an account of at least $25,000. This is not to say that working with a high level of leverage is always ideal, because it also involves a high level of risk. If you are willing to take on that risk, you will have a higher level of flexibility in executing various strategies in trading forex.

Because of the leverage, you will be able to enter into speculative trading without having to invest a lot of your own money. This type of trading is also referred to as "marginal trading." For instance, your analysis of the forex market tells you that the price of EUR will eventually rise against USD. Because of this, you decide to open one lot (or contract) to buy 10,000 units of EUR with a 1% margin, or a leverage of 1:100 at the price of 1.2760 USD per EUR (or a total of $127,600). After some time, you see that your original analysis was correct so you decide to close your position at 1.2847 (or a total of $128,470) and earn 87 pips, or a total of $870. Almost all currencies traded in the forex market fluctuate on a daily basis, with an average of one hundred to one hundred fifty pips. In some instances, the fluctuation can be even higher than that.

The foreign exchange market is perpetually moving, and as a forex trader, you can choose to keep a particular position for either a very brief period of time or for extended periods, which can be as long as several years. The amount of time to hold a particular position will actually depend on your chosen trading techniques or strategies.

Fundamental Analysis versus Technical Analysis

When you decide to start trading in the forex market, you can use quite a few techniques and strategies that will enable you to work out the market trends and make better decisions. The techniques and strategies you will learn in this book can essentially be categorized either as fundamental analysis or technical analysis.

Because of the Internet, information about the political and economic situations in different countries around the world can be readily accessed. If you want to be successful in forex trading, you need to keep yourself updated with this type of information for the reason that these events or situations can influence the general performance of the forex market. When you are well-informed, you will understand why certain currency prices change as a reaction to the events. This type of analysis is what we refer to as fundamental analysis, and it involves scrutiny of a specific country's unpredicted situations or events, including any political instability, that can cause the country's currency to hugely fluctuate.

There are certain cases when an economic forecast has been confidently made that information used in fundamental analysis turn out to be a prophecy that fulfills itself, because the market acts in response to the economic forecast even before the actual event happens, which ultimately results in the predicted outcome. The market can have an early reaction to a particular forecast in which they start buying or selling depending on what the forecast is, and when the prediction actually happens, the price of the currency will begin to move towards the opposite direction from the actual movement. This is because the forecasted outcome has already happened and the forex traders are already closing their positions. Because of this, when the actual event happens, it may seem like the forex market has an opposite reaction to what was originally predicted.

Since all of the currencies are shifting in harmony towards one direction, it will be difficult to sort through all the details that can impact the outcome. More often than not, fundamental analysis can be too overwhelming for traders who are just beginning to trade forex. It is really just the large banks and other financial institutions that are able to hire expert analysts to get into a more accurate and wider range of information on a timely basis. This is also the reason why a lot more traders are more competent when it comes to performing technical analysis.

The common premise of most technical analyses is that all the political and economic information that you need to investigate are already incorporated in the trading charts available to you. Even the predicted reactions to certain economic events can already be seen on the charts. When you do technical analysis, you study how the prices of the currencies move together with other data, such as the period of time and actual volume. You ask questions like: What is the lowest price that this particular currency attained with the past month, quarter, or year? What is the highest price? What is the average monthly volume of transactions for this particular currency?

Another premise of technical analysis is the assumption that the forex market repeats itself. This means that what happened in the past has a high likelihood of happening again in the future. Traders who perform technical analysis review currency quotes from the past and use those to predict future prices based on arithmetical and statistical computations. Fundamental analysis and technical analysis are complementary, and it is important for you to learn how to do both in order for you to succeed as a professional forex trader. At any given time, you may notice that certain elements in your fundamental analysis are also present in your technical analysis.

Chapter 2: Basics of Forex Trading

If you have started reading about forex trading, you most probably have heard the terms bid-ask or bid-offer. These terms are basically price quotes used for currency pairs. When trading forex, all currencies are paired with another currency, and the quotes that you will get are also double where one represents the quote for buying and another for selling. The difference between the two quotes or prices is what we refer to as the "spread." In this chapter, you will learn the basic procedures for trading in the forex market.

Forex Trading Positions

A lot of people enter forex trading in order to earn extra income and to diversify their existing investment portfolios. They are able to achieve these goals by taking positions to buy and sell varying sets of currencies. When the price of a currency increases after you have purchased it at a lesser price, you can earn your income when you "close" the position, or sell your currencies at a higher price. When you close your position, or the working order, you are technically putting up for sale the base currency that you originally bought, and you are purchasing its matching currency. This transaction involves a correlation of relative worth since the worth of one of the currencies in the pair is evaluated against the worth of the other currency. Because of this, a particular currency will only have its worth as a consequence of its correlation with another currency from another nation.

The "position" or "order" that you will open in the forex market will represent your net amount of exposure in a specific currency and in its corresponding currency pair. Your position can be described as "flat" when you basically have zero or no exposure, "long" if you are buying more currency than selling them, and "short" if you are selling more currency than buying them. When you start trading in forex, you are basically trading one currency for a different currency because you expect that the currency you bought will increase in value as compared to the value of the currency that you sold.

One of the basic forex concepts that you need to fully understand is that currencies are always traded in pairs. When you perform a trade, you are concurrently purchasing one currency which is the "base currency" (the 1st currency in the pair quote) and selling another currency which is the "quote currency" (the 2nd currency in the pair quote). You can make your profit a "realized income" by selling back the currency that you originally bought at an increased price, but you also have the option of holding your position and choosing to realize your income at a later period of time. In this case, you will have an "open position."

When you buy a specific currency pair, you are technically buying a specific amount of the base currency and selling the equivalent amount of the quote currency. This transaction is also referred to as "going long" or "longing the market." For instance, if you go long 100,000 units in the USD/EUR pair, it means that you are buying 100,000 units of the US dollar (the base currency) and selling the corresponding amount in Euro (the quote currency). If the price you were quote was 1.40 for USD/EUR, you are basically selling 140,000 units of the Euro. When you sell the corresponding Euro amount, you are guaranteeing the purchase of the USD counterpart.

The same rule applies to the reverse position which is also referred to as "shorting the market" or "going short." When you go short on a specific base currency, you observe that the value of the base currency is declining compared to the value of the quote currency. Because of that, you will then decide to sell, for instance, the 100,000 units of US dollars that you originally bought and purchase back the 140,000 units of Euro, because you anticipate that the value of the US dollar will eventually decline and you would want to purchase it back at a lower Euro price afterwards to realize your profits.

To summarize: a position is long when you are buying a particular currency, and a position is short when you are selling that same currency. Here is another forex trading concept you need to understand: forex quotes are also usually given as pairs of bid and ask. Long forex positions (or when you are buying a currency) apply the "ask" (offer) price in the quote. For instance, if you want to purchase one standard lot of CHF/USD at a quoted rate of 1.5722 bid/1.5727 ask, it implies that you will be purchasing 100,000 units of CHF at 1.5727 US dollar. On the other hand, short forex positions (or when you are selling a currency) will apply the "bid" price in the quote. Using the same example, that means that you will be selling 100,000 units of CHF at 1.5722 US dollars.

Forex trading involves the simultaneous and symmetrical buying and selling of currency pairs. This means that you will always be long (buying) in one particular currency and short (selling) in another corresponding currency at the same time. In the above instance, if you trade your 100,000 CHF at 1.5722 US dollars, it means that you will be short (selling) in Swiss Francs (or CHF) and long (buying) in US dollars.

When you choose to keep your position open (running or active), it means that its worth will always vary depending on how the market rates fluctuate. Your position may have profits when the prices go up or losses when the prices go down, but those profits and loss will not be final or realized until you decide to close your position.

How to Trade on Margin

You can compare trading on margin by opening a loan account from a banking institution or broker that can enable you to buy certain currency pairs. The margin that you will need depends on the leverage that the bank or other financial institutions can offer, and it will represent the guarantee that you need to provide in order to gain control over a certain volume of currency units.

For instance, if you are given a 100:1 leverage, it means that you can control a $100,000 lot or contract with only a $1,000 margin or investment in your forex account. Other forex companies offer lots in smaller sizes to allow new investors to join the forex market. A small lot size will normally allow you to control a $10,000 lot with only a $100 margin or investment.

Let me warn you about forex accounts that provide you with extremely high leverages. These high leverages may permit you to manage a higher volume of currencies in the forex market with a lower margin or investment from your end, but they can also be very risky especially when you start experiencing losses. Because your margin or investment is minimal, you may be tempted to enter positions or transactions that have extreme high risks. You may think that your investment is small and you are willing to lose all of them. That is a good investment mentality, but remember your primary objective in trading forex, which is to earn money in the long run.

Whether you are working with a low or high margin, it is ideal for you to learn how to manage your forex position properly. You need to set "stop-loss" and "target-profit levels" that will enable you to successfully manage the positions that you open. You will learn more about these strategies in the next chapter.

How to Close a Forex Position

When you open a forex position, you can also activate a feature that will allow your account to automatically close the position when it has reached a certain condition that you have specified. These conditions can include target-profit (when your position has reached a certain profit level) or stop-loss (when your position has reached a certain level of loss). You can also choose to manually close your position by logging into your online account or by contacting your broker. When you choose to perform manual closing of your position, you will be subjected to similar conditions that apply when you open a position at market price.

What are Pips and Lots?

As we have mentioned earlier, a point or pip (derived from "Percentage In Point") is the smallest unit of currency movements. A pip represents a 0.0001 variation (either increase or decrease) in currency pairs based on four decimals and a 0.01 variation in currency pairs based on two decimals. For instance, when the price of CHF/USD increases from 1.3740 to 1.3799, it means that the price increased by 59 pips.

Different currency pairs have different pip values which are fundamentally founded on the correlation between the changing currency rates. The computation of a pip is different where EUR is the base currency (such as EUR/USD) compared to a currency pair where EUR is the quote currency (e.g. USD/EUR).

The price movements of currencies are normally gauged by the number of pips. A price movement of one pip is equivalent to a certain amount of profits or losses in real US dollar in each forex trade. Normally, the rate of a pip varies based on the particular currency pairs that are being traded. The rate of a pip will only be similar for currency pairs that have USD as the quote currency (the 2nd currency in the pair). The reason for this is that whatever the base currency is (whether EUR, CHF or AUD), the USD quote currency will always fluctuate at the same rate.

To establish the amount of your profit or loss on a specific trade, you need to first know the rate of the pip and then use that rate to multiply the total number of pips that the currency has moved for or counter to your position. If the price of the base currency increased compared to the price of the quote currency, every pip that the price increased above your original purchase price can be considered as a gain or profit. On the other hand, each pip that price decreased below the original purchase price can be considered as a loss.

It is particularly imperative for you to always remember that if the quote currency is USD (such as CHF/USD), the rate of one pip will always be equal to 0.0001 US dollar or 1/100 of a cent for each US dollar that you trade. This means that the rate of a pip for a standard lot of USD 100,000 is USD 10 and USD 1 for a smaller sized lot of USD 10,000. The rates of a pip for other currency pairs can range from USD 0.00006 to USD 0.00009. This means that a standard lot of USD 100,000 can have a USD 6 to USD 9 pip. Here are a few sample computations that can help you better understand how pips are computed:

US Dollar as the Base Currency

- USD/CHF. If the currency value is equal to 1.1819, the pip value can be computed as 0.0001 divided by 1.1819 or 0.0000846095. Since a standard lot has 100,000 units, the total pip value is equivalent to $8.46 (computed as 0.0000846095 multiplied by 100,000).

- USD/JPY. If the currency value is equal to 92.39, the pip value can be computed as 0.01 divided by 92.29 or 0.0001082368. With a standard lot of 100,000 units, the total pip value is equivalent to $10.82 (computed as 0.0001082368 multiplied by 100,000).

USD Dollar as the Quote Currency

- EUR/USD. If the currency value is equal to 1.2658, the pip value in Euro can be computed as 0.0001 divided by 1.2758 or 0.000078. You can compute for the pip value in US dollar as 0.000078 multiplied by 1.2758 or 0.0001. With a standard lot of 100,000 units, the total pip value is equivalent to $10 (computed as 0.0001 multiplied by 100,000).

- No matter what the base currency is (CHF, AUD, or NZD), the ultimate pip value will always be $10.

The most common order types are market orders and limit orders. You can enter or exit a particular trade position by issuing a "market order" that will allow you to purchase or sell your currencies at present market prices. You need to be extra cautious when issuing market orders, because the forex market can move so fast that the market price at the time your market order is issued and at the actual time of the completion of the buy or sell transaction may vary. This variance is also referred to as "slippage" and can happen in a matter of just a few minutes or even seconds. A slippage can have a potential impact on your transaction, which can result in you losing or gaining a number of pips. Slippage is normally avoided when you transact your forex trading online, because the execution or completion of your market order can be completed instantaneously or in a just a few seconds depending on the speed of your Internet.

You can place a "limit order" which can allow you to automatically buy or sell a particular currency when its price reaches a specific level or limit. For instance, you can place a limit order that will automatically buy a currency when its market price drops below the "limit-order price" that you set, or you can automatically sell a currency when its market price becomes higher than the limit-order price that you set. Slippage risk does not occur with limit orders because your order is technically generated by the computer. Forex traders normally place a limit order when they anticipate that the market price of a currency will eventually recover after a certain economic or political event.

Chapter 3: Forex Trading Strategies

The most common forex trading techniques can be categorized into two broad groups: long-term trading and short-term trading. With long-term trading, a trader bases his or her analysis on end-of-day data and charts and can decide to maintain a position for several weeks, or even months. What a long-term trader basically does is monitor the trends. One of the advantages of long-term forex trading is that you wouldn't have to monitor the forex market several times during the day, and you would have to complete a lesser number of trade transactions, which translates to lesser commission fees or charges. Additionally, you would also not need to use elaborate equipment or computer software to help in your trend analysis because you would not really spend a lot of time with the analysis and monitoring of the market trends.

Two of the biggest disadvantages of longer-term trading are the requirement to establish bigger stops and the risk of huge equity swings. As a long-term trader, you will have to be well-capitalized so you can be more primed to face those huge equity swings. Because you will only perform several trade transactions in a month, you need to have a lot of patience, especially during months or weeks when you are on the losing end and you are waiting for the market prices to pick up.

With short-term forex trading, a trader will base his or her analysis on intraday data and information and will usually maintain a forex position for just a couple of days or, at most, up to two weeks. The kind of forex trading that short-term traders do is called "swing trading". There are also traders who perform an even shorter form of forex trading called "day trading," where they aim to earn small profits because of price swings that happen within the day. One of the biggest benefits of short-term trading is that you will be able to take advantage of the numerous trading opportunities that happen every day. When you are able to earn even a small amount of profit every day, you have a lesser chance of experiencing any losing months. You will not have to depend on one or two major forex trades that you perform once a year to earn a profit. The biggest drawback of short-term trading is the higher transaction fees or charges that you would be incurring.

Here are the most common trading techniques you can employ to earn profits from forex trading. Carefully read each one and determine which strategy matches your investment objectives and personality type:

1. Scalping

The primary objective in the scalping forex strategy is to earn small amounts of profit in frequent intervals from minute price movements that can range from two to ten pips. With scalping, you can enter and exit a particular trade within a couple of minutes, or even mere seconds. The small profits that you earn from scalping can eventually add up to a bigger profit because you will be able to enter into a high number of transactions within a day that can range from twenty to one hundred transactions on average.

Many expert traders consider scalping a very risky forex trading strategy, but the level of risk involved in scalping can vary depending on both the actual time of the day you complete your transactions and the forex market that you use. You are more likely to become successful in scalping during trending conditions, and the most ideal trading time is when the forex market is varying within consolidation patterns. When you want to implement the scalping strategy, you need to make sure that you will be able to react and make decisions in a fast manner so that you can get out of a bad trade as soon as you can with minimal pip loss. Because scalping will allow you to take numerous forex trades within the day, you should take any profit opportunities that are presented to you, even if they are a very small amount. You should not aim for a profit that is outside five to ten pips in order to maximize your efforts in scalping.

2. Intraday Trading

When you implement intraday or day forex trading, you will need to close all your positions before the end of the day. With this strategy, the number of transactions that you will close is expected to be much less than the scalping strategy. You will normally analyze a trade and complete it within a short or medium timeframe that involves charts with a thirty minute to an hour timeframe.

3. Position Trading

With the position trading strategy, the objective is to improve your position size in increments as you observe the market evolution to make sure that you are able to maintain a constant level of risk. This technique is also referred to as "averaging into a position," where you will open a new forex position of a similar size and direction each time the risks of the previous position can already be covered.

Let us say that you purchase a 0.10 lot of currency pair CHF/USD at 1.2650 and establish your stop-loss at 1.2600. That means that your open risk is $50.

Lot No.	Price	Stop-Loss	Open Risk	Potential Profit
1st	1.2650	1.2600	$50	0

When the currency price increases, you will then purchase a second mini-lot at 1.2700 with a stop-loss at 1.2650, which will make the stop-loss of the first position at a breakeven point of 1.2650. After opening the second position, your overall risk is still at $50.

Lot No.	Price	Stop-Loss	Open Risk	Potential Profit
1st	1.2650	1.2650	0	0
2nd	1.2700	1.2650	$50	0

If the currency prices keep on increasing, you can purchase a third mini-lot at 1.2750 with a stop-loss at 1.2700 and keep the stop-loss of the first and second positions both at 1.2700.

Lot No.	Price	Stop-Loss	Open Risk	Potential Profit
1st	1.2650	1.2700	0	$50
2nd	1.2700	1.2700	0	0

3rd	1.2750	1.2700	$50	0

Now, you may be wondering if you should stop at the third mini-lot because with that, all three of your mini-lots now have a breakeven position. If you observe that the market price continues to rise, you can continue with your purchase of a fourth mini-lot at 1.2800 with a stop-loss at 1.2750, which can then guard your profits for all four mini-lots.

Lot No.	Price	Stop-Loss	Open Risk	Potential Profit
1st	1.2650	1.2750	0	$100
2nd	1.2700	1.2750	0	$50
3rd	1.2750	1.2750	0	0
4th	1.2800	1.2750	$50	0

You can proceed to buying your fifth lot at 1.2850 with a stop-loss at 1.2800, and with that, your secured profits will amount to $250, which is computed as $150 from the first lot, plus $100 from the second lot, plus $50 from the third lot, minus the $50 risk exposure on the fifth lot. The fourth lot will be at a breakeven point.

Lot No.	Price	Stop-Loss	Open Risk	Potential Profit
1st	1.2650	1.2800	0	$150

2nd	1.2700	1.2800	0	$100
3rd	1.2750	1.2800	0	$50
4th	1.2800	1.2800	0	0
5th	1.2850	1.2800	$50	0

With position trading, you can control your risks and exposures because you will be able to maintain them at the same level throughout the process, and you have the potential to accrue high profits. With this strategy, you will be able to keep up with the market trends. This is ideal if you have a longer investment timeline. You can also implement the concept of position trading even if you are doing intraday forex trading. Within a particular day, you can add to your position in the same manner explained above so you can collect the profits at the end of the day with minimum risk. You need to keep in mind that you should try out the position trading strategy with small lot sizes, and make sure that your risk exposure is limited to 1% to 2% of your total capital investment. That means if your forex account investment is $1,000, your exposure should be limited to $10 to $20 only.

Chapter 4: How to Create a Trading Plan

Now that you know the basics of forex trading and the techniques you can use, it is now time for you to create a trading plan. Creating a trading plan will not provide you with a 100% guarantee that you will become a successful forex trader, but with a trading plan, you will be able to avoid grave mistakes or find a solution when those mistakes do happen. A trading plan will provide you with the required tools that will enable you to quickly react to any possible trading results. With a trading plan, you will be able to create a clear sequence of steps that you need to go through while trading, which can enable you to control emotions and create discipline. Here are the elements of a good trading plan on which you need to decide:

- Market: What currencies do you intend to buy or sell (EUR/USD, CHF/JPY)?

- Position size: How much volume do you intend to buy or sell?

- Risks: How much of your capital investment can you risk losing?

- Entry: When you do intend to start buying or selling? What market hours or news releases do you want to follow?

- Stop: When do you intend to close a position that is losing money?

- Exit: When do you intend to close a position that is earning profits?

- Strategy: What strategy do you want to use in buying or selling? What primary and secondary indicators will you implement?

- Time frame: How much profit do you expect to earn from a particular position?

- Breakeven point: What is the breakeven point for this particular position?

Here are the steps you need to take before opening a forex position:

1. Determine the previous daily activities of the particular forex position that you want to open. Are the prices not yet congested or over-extended? Are the current prices near the highs and lows of the prior day? Read the news and any economic reports available on the Internet. Check for any potential gaps that happened during the weekend or a previous holiday.

2. Determine the price bar of the position you want to enter so you can predict the prospective direction of the price trend.

Long (Buying) – Alternative 1

The price trend is going up with a down swing that is higher than the two prior downswings.

Long (Buying) – Alternative 2

The secondary price trend is falling down, but rises up in a direction similar to the primary price trend.

Long (Buying) – Alternative 3

The secondary price trend is falling down, but rises up in a direction similar to the slope of the moving average price trend.

Short (Selling) – Alternative 1

The price trend is going down with an upswing that is higher than the two prior upswings.

Short (Selling) – Alternative 2

The secondary price trend is rising up, but goes down a direction similar to the primary price trend.

Short (Selling) – Alternative 3

The secondary price trend is rising up, but goes down in a direction similar to the slope of the moving average price trend.

3. Decide on your entry prices:

- Buy entry price: Purchase currencies when the market price is over the high level of the signal bar + one tick.

- Sell entry price: Sell your currencies when the price is under the low level of the signal bar – one tick.

4. Decide on your exit strategy. Remember that your goal is to take profits.

Alternative 1: with 1 mini lot Strategy

Exit when your profit hits around 60% of the average price range.

Alternative 2: with 2 mini lot Strategy

Exit one lot if you have earned a full profit. Trail the stop of the second mini-lot.

Alternative 3: with 3 mini lot Strategy

Exit one lot if you have earned a full profit. Trail the stops of the second and third mini-lots. Keep the last two lots open until you see a reversal signal or when the trading session for the day has ended.

Mindset of a Forex Trader

Here is another trading concept you need to understand: it is possible that you will not always earn profit from your forex trades every day. There will be days when you will earn more than your target and days when you will actually lose money. That is where the trading plan comes in. If you fail to thoroughly plan for a particular trade, it is highly probable that it will be improper, even if you think that the results are positive. Ironically, if you adhere to your trade plan, your trade will be proper, even if they result in a temporary loss, because you stuck to your own plan and strategy.

Another vital aspect of a trading plan that you need to remember is that you need to maintain a comprehensive record of all your forex trades, whether you earned profits on those trades or lost money. You need to jot down details such as entry and exit prices, the actual time and date, your actual stops and targeted stops, and so forth. You also need to take into account the emotional aspect of your trades. What was your emotional status during that time? What were your primary reasons for starting the trade?

Keeping a trading log can help you review your past transactions and identify any weak areas that need to be corrected, as well as strong areas of which you can take advantage. If you do not keep a log, you will just be dangling in the hands of "Lady Luck," and you will not know the reasons for your successes and failures, which would be just like pure blind gambling.

Conclusion

I hope this book was able to help you to better understand how forex trading works and the strategies that can help you earn income that can bring you closer to your financial freedom.

The next step is to install a simulation tool you can get from the Internet for free so you can try your hands on forex trading without risking your own money.

On a final note, if you enjoyed this book, please take the time to share your thoughts and post a review on Amazon. It'd be greatly appreciated.

Finally, we would like to ask you to give a short, honest, and unbiased review of this book.

Please & Thank you!

Instant Access to Free Book Package!

As a thank you for the purchase of this book, I want to offer you some more material. We collaborate with multiple other authors specializing in various fields. We have best-selling, master writers in history, biographies, DIY projects, home improvement, arts & crafts and much more! **We make a promise to you to deliver at least 4 books a week in different genres, a value of $20-30, for FREE!**

All you need to do is sign up your email here at http://nextstopsuccess.net/freebooks/ to join our Book Club. You will get weekly notification for more free books, courtesy of the First Class Book Club.

As a special thank you, we don't want you to wait until next week for these 4 free books. We want to give you 4 **RIGHT NOW**.

Here's what you will be getting:

- A fitness book called "BOSU Workout Routine Made Easy!"
- A book on Jim Rohn, a master life coach: "The Best of Jim Rohn: Lessons for Life Changing Success"
- A detailed biography on Conan O'Brien, a favorite late night TV show host.
- A World War 2 Best Selling box set (2 books in 1!): "The Third Reich: Nazi Rise & Fall + World War 2: The Untold Secrets of Nazi Germany".

To get instant access to this free ebook package (a value of $25), and weekly free material, all you need to do is click the link below:

http://nextstopsuccess.net/freebooks/

Add us on Facebook: First Class Book Club